Easy Piano

Playing THE Blues

33 hot songs for Gettin' Good 'n' Low Down

ISBN 0-7935-5847-6

A JOINT PUBLICATION OF

MCA
music publishing

A DIVISION OF MCA INC.
7777 W. BLUEMOUND RD. MILWAUKEE, WI 53213
AND

HAL•LEONARD™
CORPORATION

The Hottest Music of the '90s Is THE Blues

4	Baby, Won't You Please Come Home		72	Mean Old World
7	Boogie Chillen No. 2		78	Memphis Blues
10	Boom Boom (Out Go the Lights)		84	Milk Cow Blues
13	Checkin' Up on My Baby		75	Mule Kicking in My Stall
16	Chicago Blues		90	My Baby Left Me
21	Crazy Blues		92	Pinetop's Blues
30	Diving Duck		100	Rock Me Baby
26	Down Hearted Blues		102	Saint James Infirmary
37	Everyday (I Have the Blues)		104	Smokestack Lightning
42	Fine and Mellow		95	St. Louis Blues
50	A Good Man Is Hard to Find		106	Sugar Blues
47	Heartbreak Hotel		109	Tain't Nobody's Biz-ness If I Do
54	Help Me		118	The Thrill Is Gone
58	I'm a Man		114	Tobacco Road
61	In the Evening (When the Sun Goes Down)		124	West End Blues
64	It's a Low Down Dirty Shame		121	Why I Sing the Blues
67	Mad About Him, Sad Without Him, How Can I Be Glad Without Him Blues			

BABY, WON'T YOU PLEASE COME HOME

Words and Music by CHARLES WARFIELD
and CLARENCE WILLIAMS

5

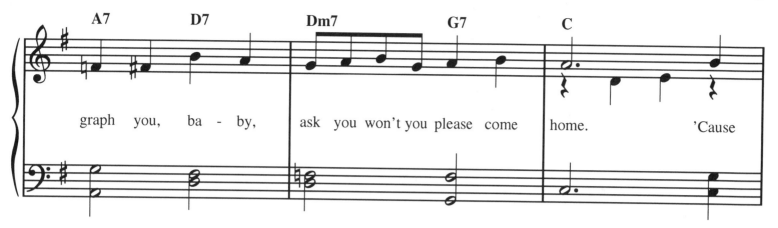

graph you, ba - by, ask you won't you please come home. 'Cause

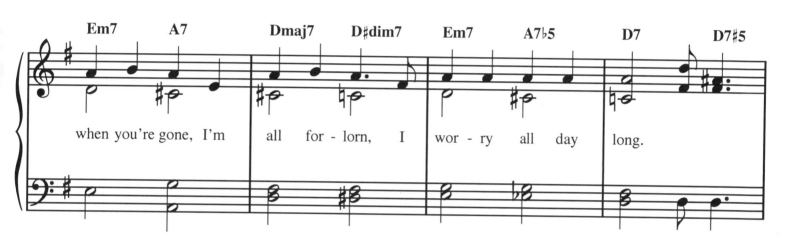

when you're gone, I'm all for - lorn, I wor - ry all day long.

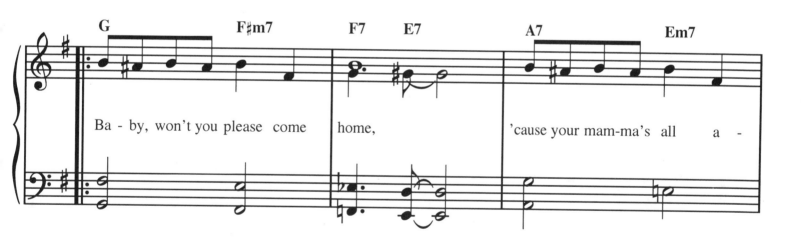

Ba - by, won't you please come home, 'cause your mam-ma's all a -

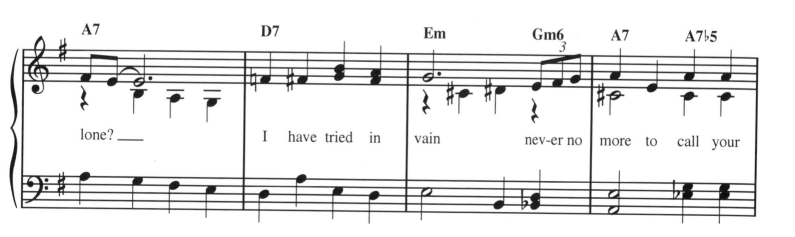

lone? ___ I have tried in vain nev-er no more to call your

BOOGIE CHILLEN NO. 2

Words and Music by JOHN LEE HOOKER
and BERNARD BESMAN

BOOM BOOM
(Out Go The Lights)

By STAN LEWIS

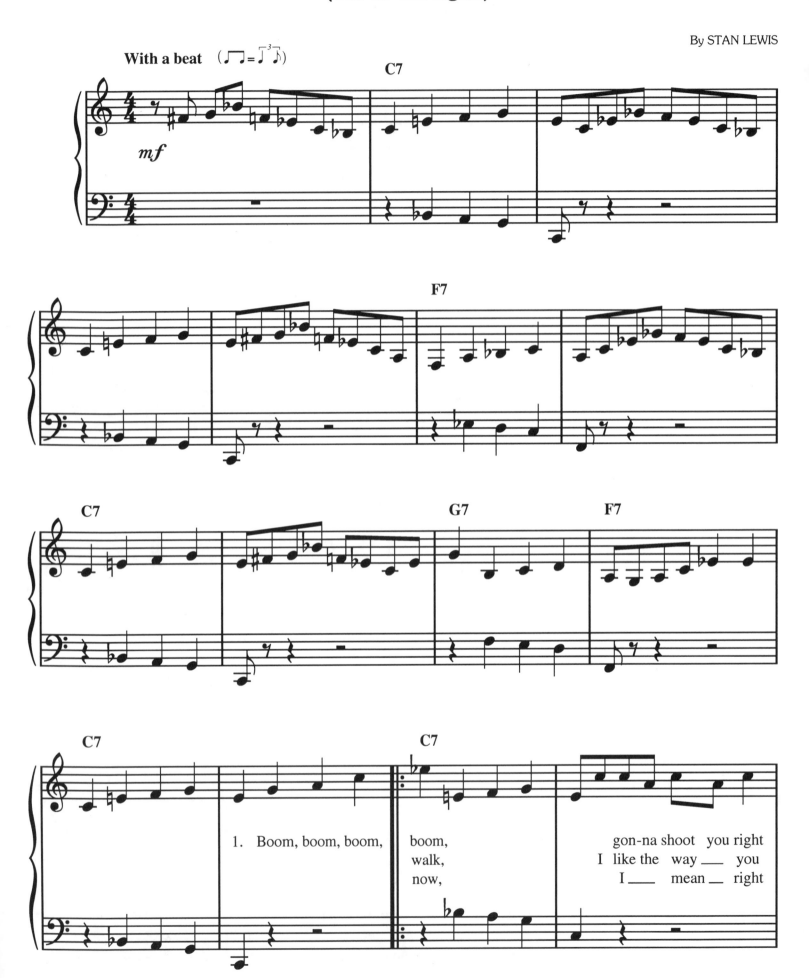

CHECKIN' UP ON MY BABY

By SONNY BOY WILLIAMSON

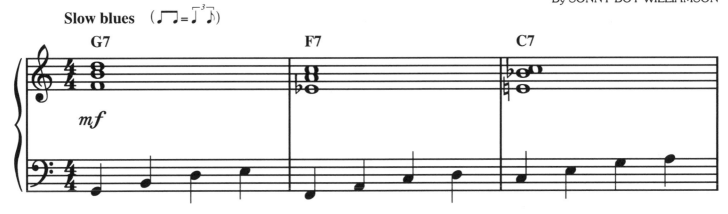

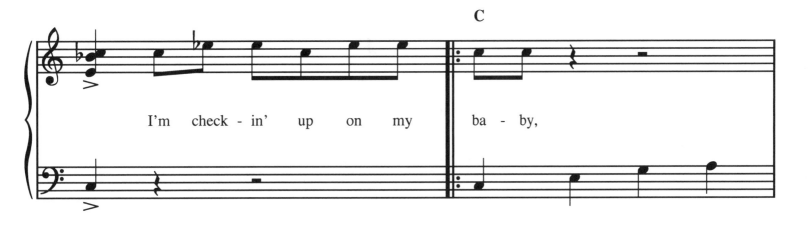

I'm check - in' up on my ba - by,

find out what she's put - tin' down.

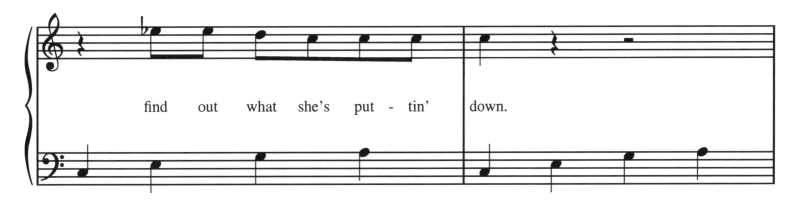

Check - in' up on my ba - by,

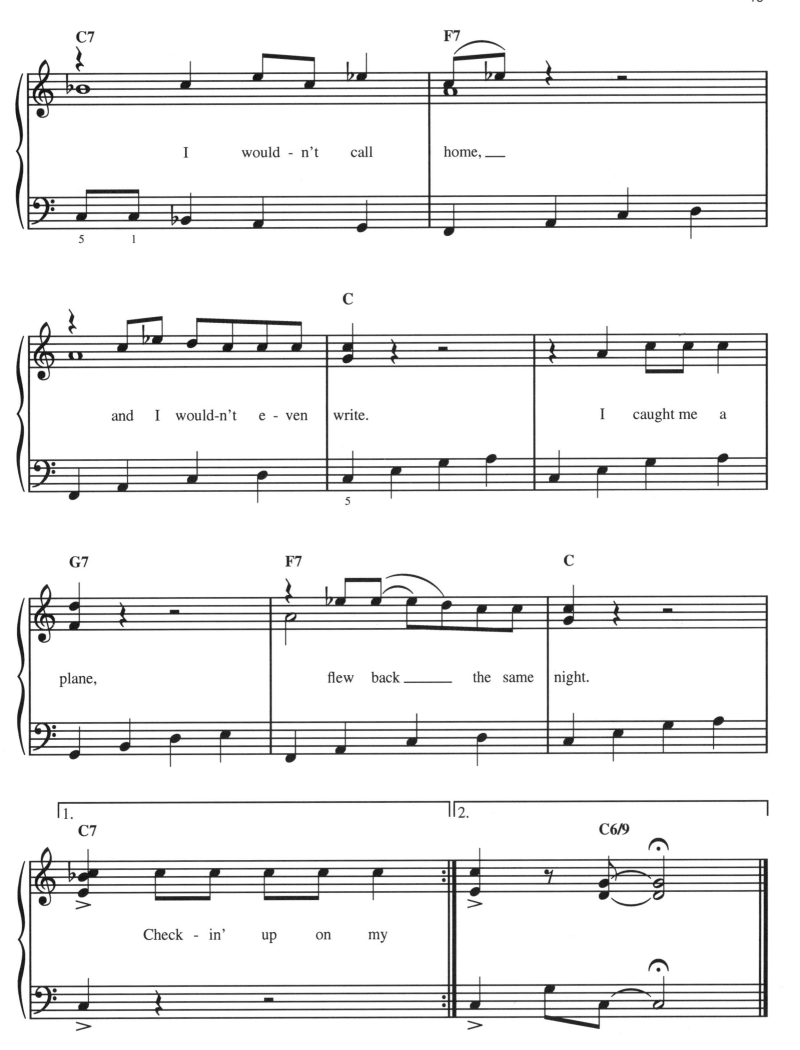

CHICAGO BLUES

Words and Music by
LONNIE JOHNSON

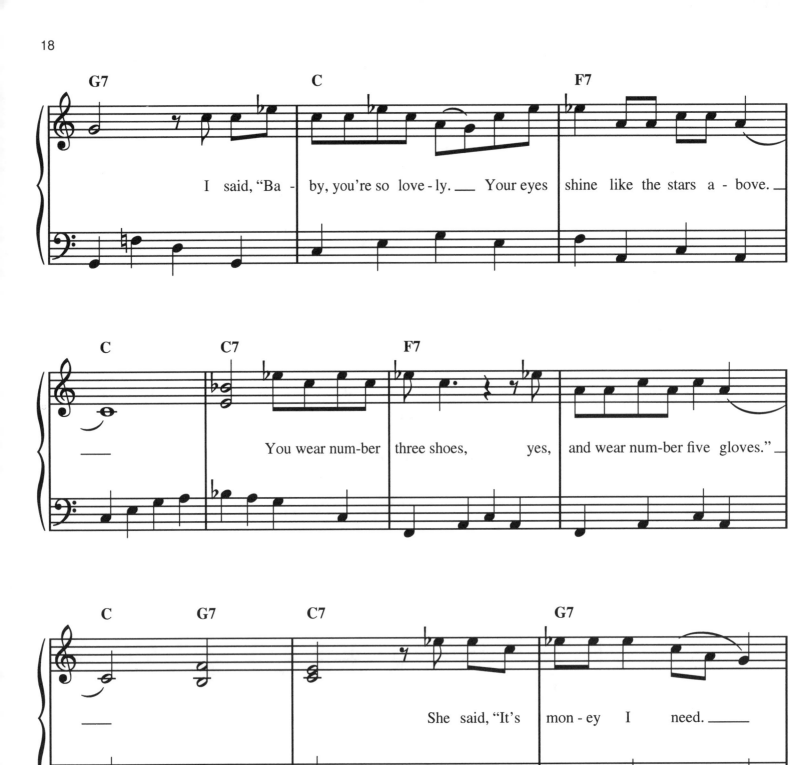

I said, "Ba - by, you're so love - ly. __ Your eyes shine like the stars a - bove.

__ You wear num - ber three shoes, yes, and wear num - ber five gloves."

She said, "It's mon - ey I need. ___

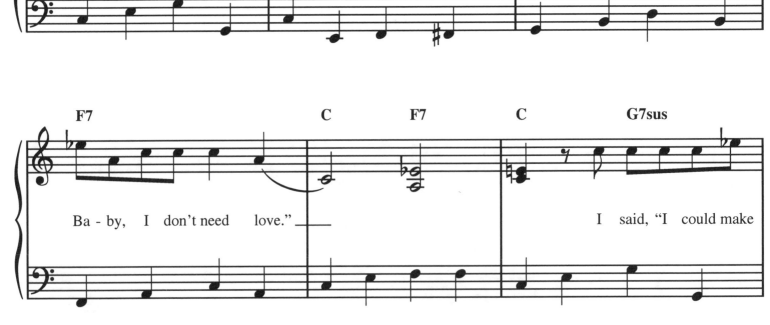

Ba - by, I don't need love." ___ I said, "I could make

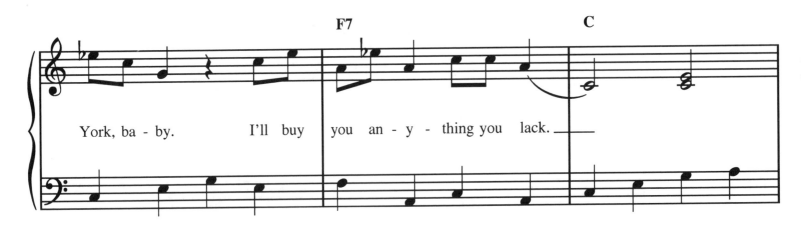

York, ba - by.   I'll buy   you an - y - thing you   lack. ___

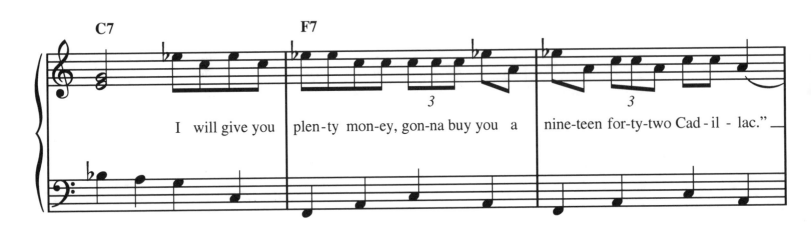

I   will give you   plen-ty mon-ey, gon-na buy you   a   nine-teen for-ty-two Cad - il - lac." ___

___   She says, "I'm   sor - ry. ___ This fine   round

bod - y   will   be   here when you get   back."

CRAZY BLUES

Words and Music by
PERRY BRADFORD

MCA music publishing

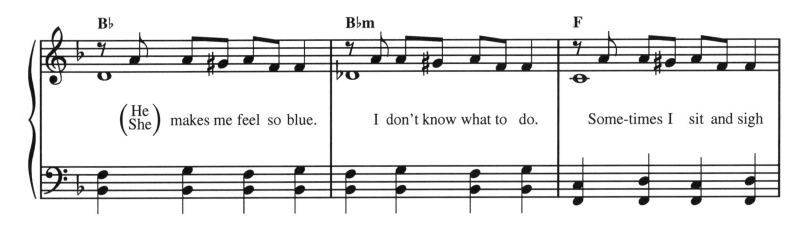

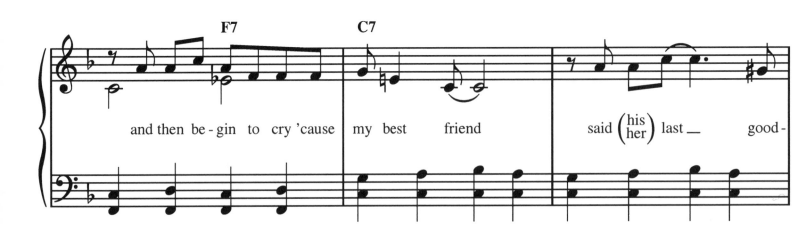

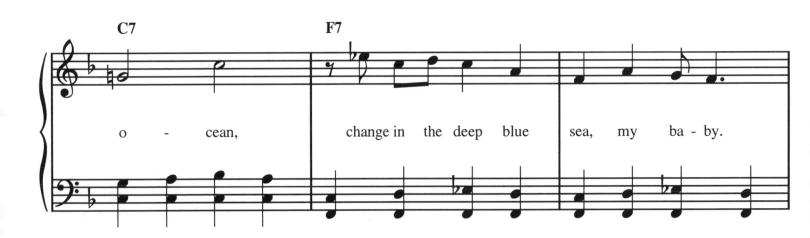

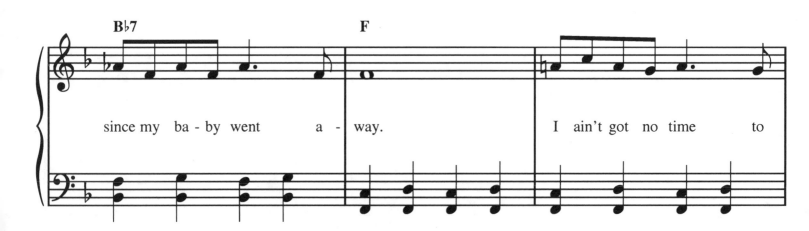

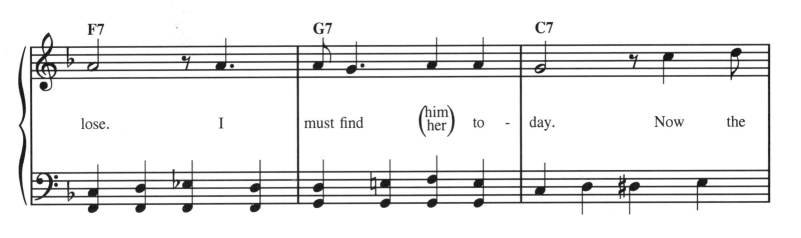

lose.   I   must find (him/her) to - day.   Now   the

doc-tor's gon-na do all   that he   can, __   but   what you're gon-na need is   an

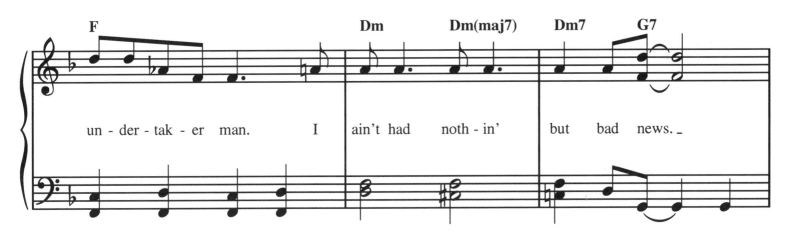

un - der - tak - er   man.   I   ain't had   noth - in'   but   bad   news. __

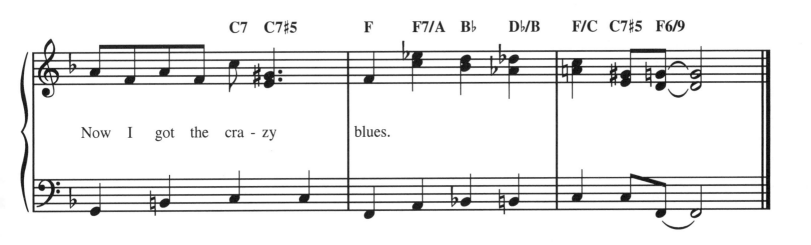

Now   I   got the cra - zy   blues.

DOWN HEARTED BLUES

Words by ALBERTA HUNTER
Music by LOVIE AUSTIN

MCA music publishing

28

seems that trou - ble's   going to fol - low me to my   grave. __
hold it, ba - by,   till you come un - der my com - mand. __

Got the
Say, I

Additional lyrics

3. Say, I ain't never loved but three $\left(\begin{array}{c}\text{men}\\\text{women}\end{array}\right)$ in my life.

    No, I ain't never loved but three $\left(\begin{array}{c}\text{men}\\\text{women}\end{array}\right)$ in my life,

    'Twas my $\left(\begin{array}{c}\text{father, brother}\\\text{mother, sister}\end{array}\right)$ and the $\left(\begin{array}{c}\text{man}\\\text{woman}\end{array}\right)$ who wrecked my life.

4. 'Cause $\left(\begin{array}{c}\text{he}\\\text{she}\end{array}\right)$ mistreated me and $\left(\begin{array}{c}\text{he}\\\text{she}\end{array}\right)$ drove me from $\left(\begin{array}{c}\text{his}\\\text{her}\end{array}\right)$ door,

    Yes, $\left(\begin{array}{c}\text{he}\\\text{she}\end{array}\right)$ mistreated me and $\left(\begin{array}{c}\text{he}\\\text{she}\end{array}\right)$ drove me from $\left(\begin{array}{c}\text{his}\\\text{her}\end{array}\right)$ door,

    But the Good Book says you'll reap just what you sow.

5. Oh, it may be a week and it may be a month or two,
    Yes, it may be a week and it may be a month or two,
    But the day you quit me honey, it's coming home to you.

6. Oh, I walked the floor and I wrung my hands and cried,
    Yes, I walked the floor and I wrung my hands and cried,
    Had the down hearted blues and couldn't be satisfied.

DIVING DUCK

Words and Music by
OTIS SPANN

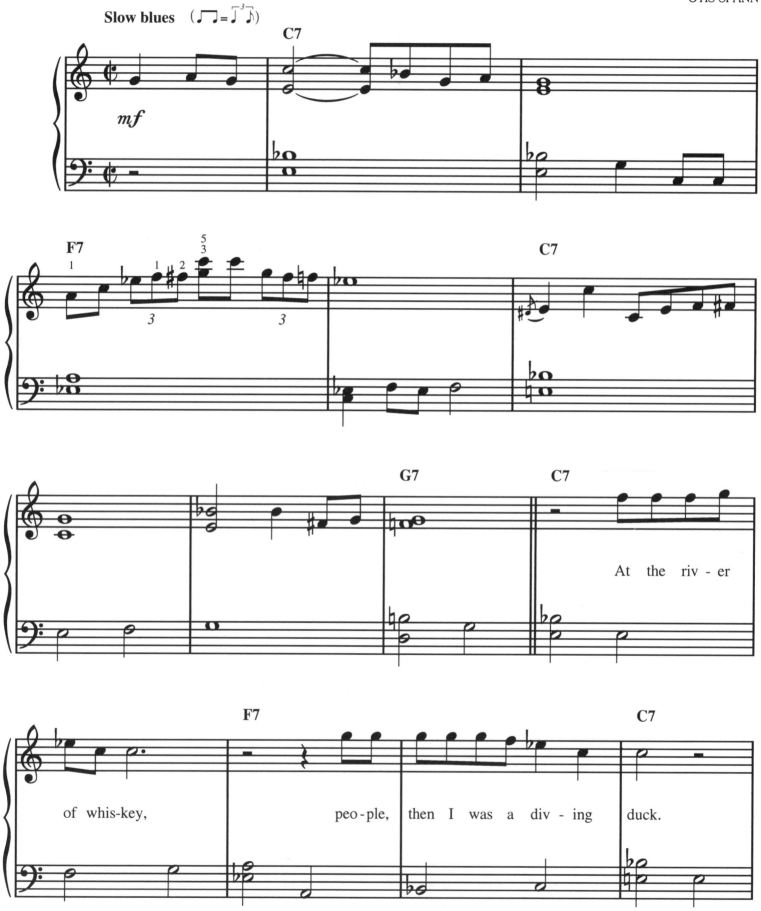

At the riv-er of whis - key, _____ peo - ple, then I was a div - ing duck. _____

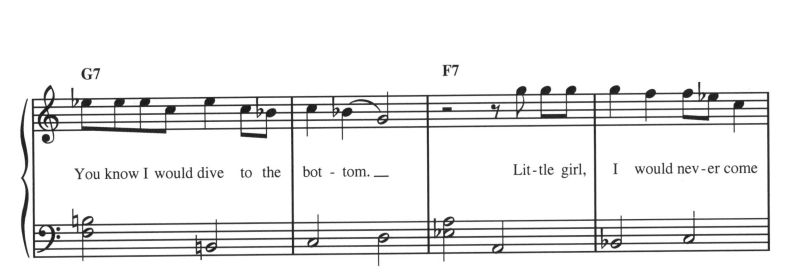

You know I would dive to the bot - tom. _____ Lit-tle girl, I would nev-er come

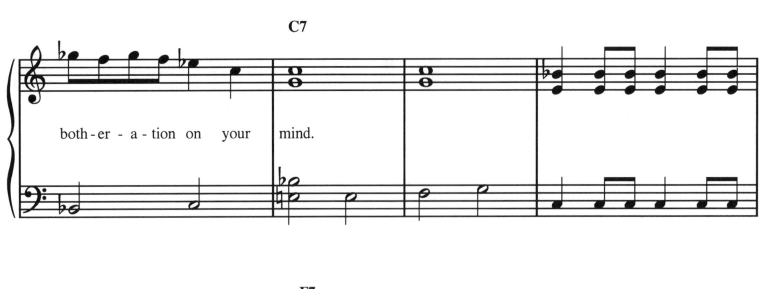

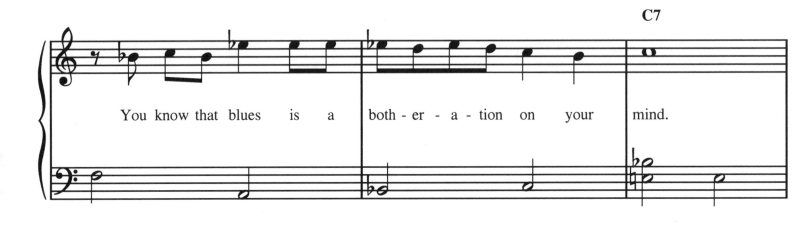

me, wom-an, oh you were leav - ing all _____ the time. _____

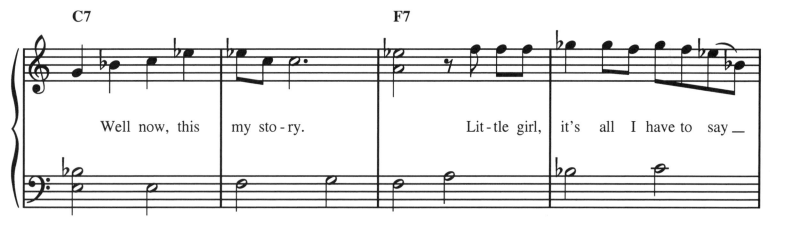

Well now, this my sto-ry. Lit-tle girl, it's all I have to say _

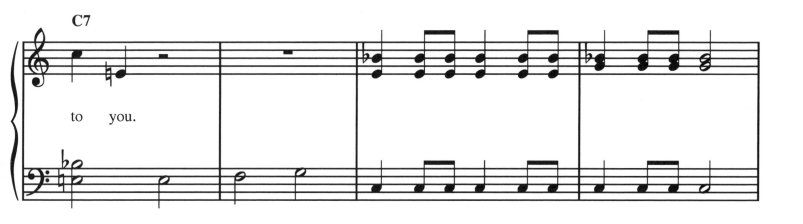

to you.

36

Oh, you know this my sto - ry. This is all I have to say to

you.

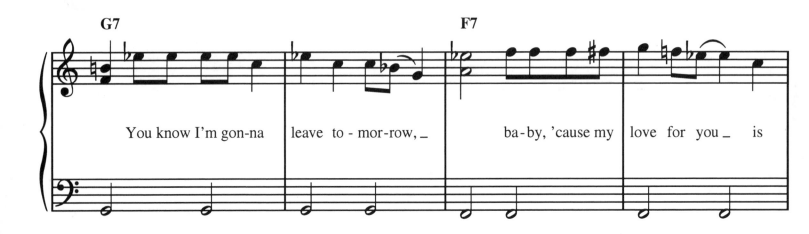

You know I'm gon-na leave to - mor-row, ba-by, 'cause my love for you is

through.

EVERYDAY
(I Have The Blues)

By PETER CHATMAN

be-cause it's you I hate to lose. _____ No-bod - y

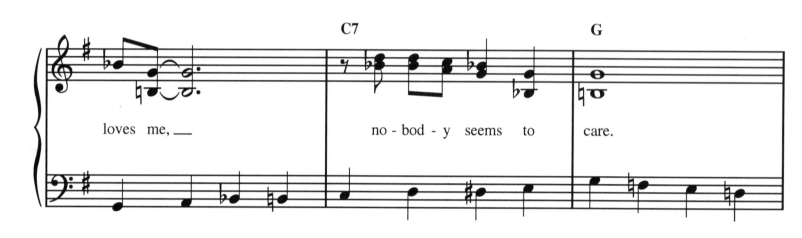

loves me, __ no - bod - y seems to care.

No-bod - y loves me, no-bod - y seems to __ care.

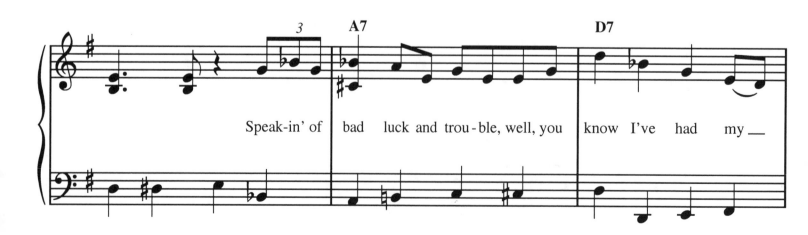

Speak-in' of bad luck and trou - ble, well, you know I've had my __

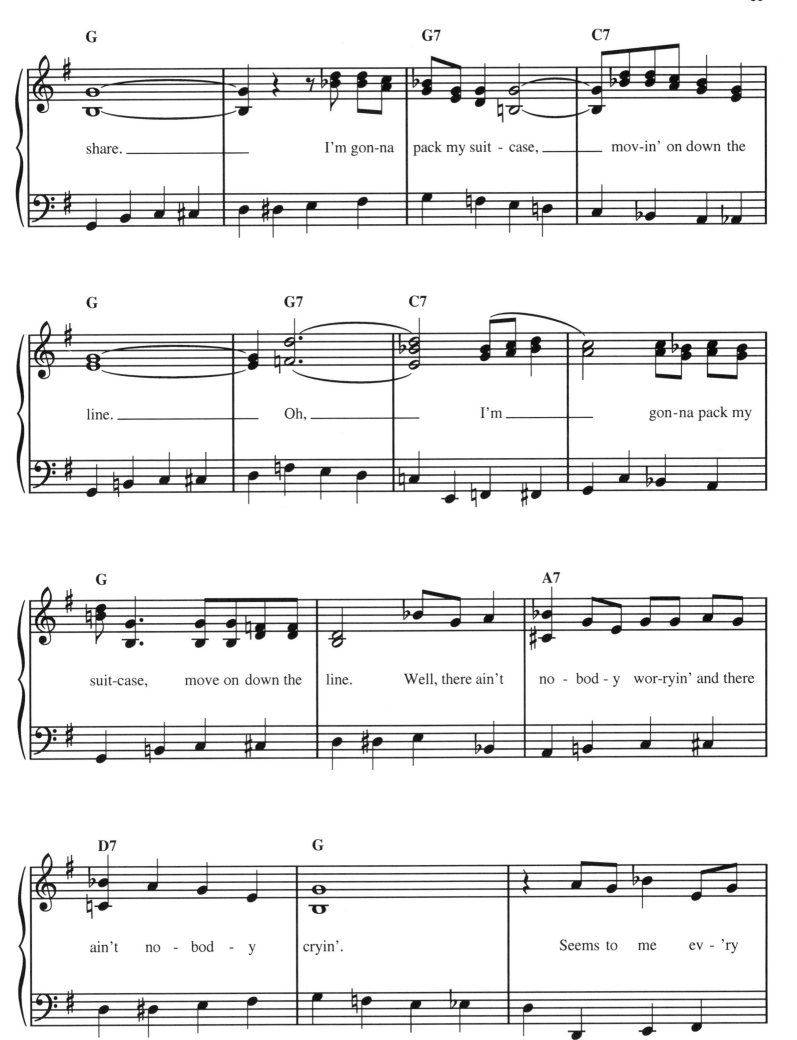

day, ev-'ry day, ev'ry day I have the blues.

G7   **C7**

Ev-'ry day, ev-'ry day, ev-'ry day, ev-'ry day I have the

G   **Am7**

blues.   You see me wor-ry, ba-by, 'cause it's

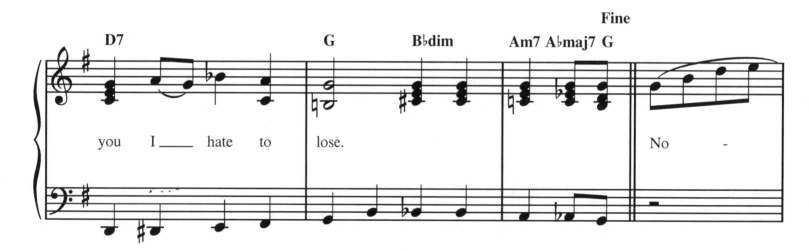

D7   **G**   **Bbdim**   **Am7 Abmaj7 G**   **Fine**

you I ___ hate to lose.   No -

D.S. al Fine

FINE AND MELLOW

Words and Music by
BILLIE HOLIDAY

lowest man that I've ever seen.

He wears high draped pants, stripes are really yel-

low. He wears high draped pants,

stripes are really yel-low. But when he starts in to love me,

44

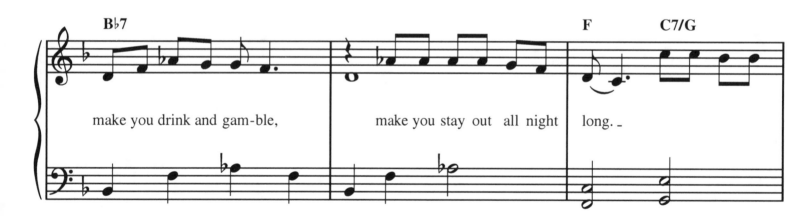

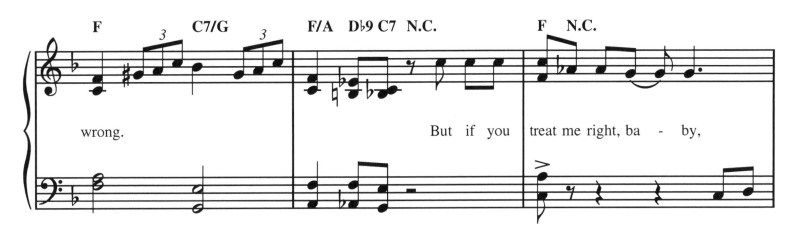

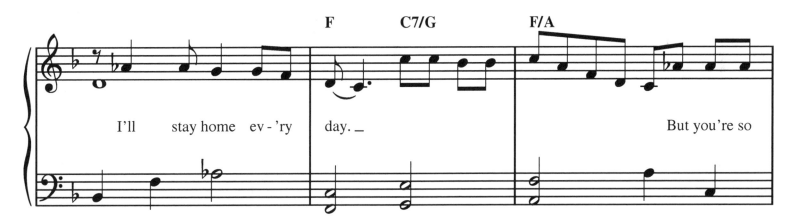

Love is   just like a fau-cet;   it turns off and

on. _   Love is like a fau-cet;   it turns off _ and

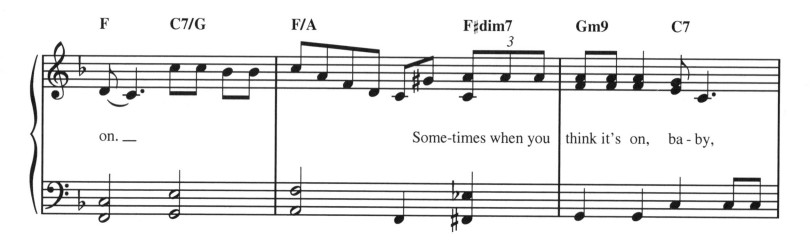

on. _   Some-times when you think it's on, ba-by,

it has turned off and gone.

HEARTBREAK HOTEL

Words and Music by MAE BOREN AXTON,
TOMMY DURDEN and ELVIS PRESLEY

1. Since my ba-by left me, I found a new place to dwell. Well, it's
   if your ba-by leaves ya, and you've got a tale to tell, well, just

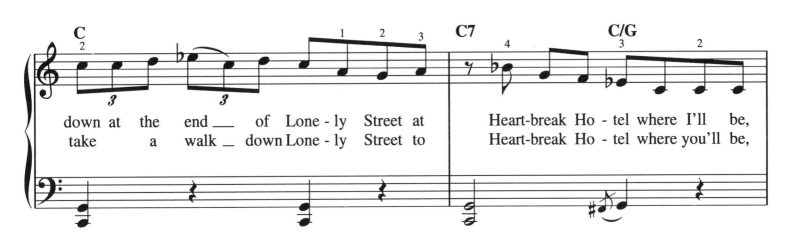

down at the end ___ of Lone-ly Street at Heart-break Ho-tel where I'll be,
take a walk ___ down Lone-ly Street to Heart-break Ho-tel where you'll be,

A GOOD MAN IS HARD TO FIND

Words and Music by
EDDIE GREEN

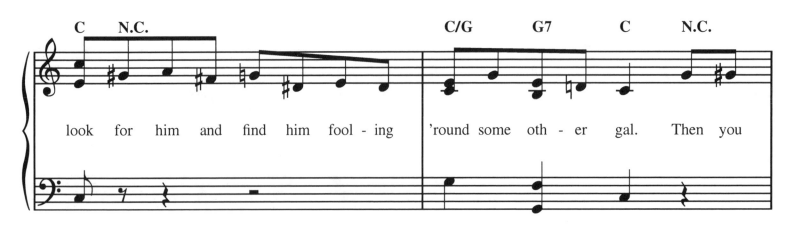

look for him and find him fool - ing 'round some oth - er gal. Then you

rave, _____ you e - ven crave _____ to see him lay - ing in his

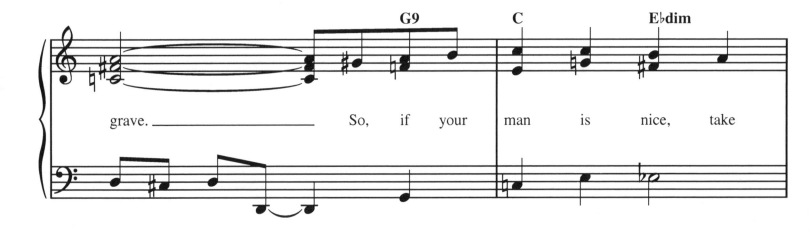

grave. _____ So, if your man is nice, take

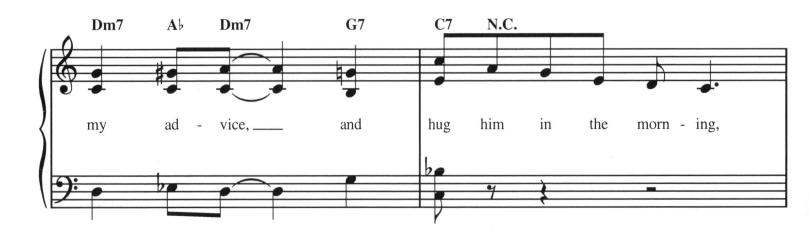

my ad - vice, ____ and hug him in the morn - ing,

HELP ME

By SONNY BOY WILLIAMSON
and RALPH BASS

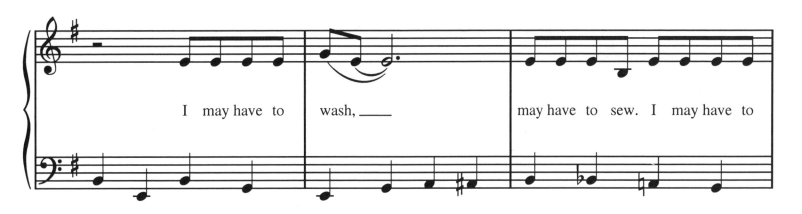

I may have to wash, _____ may have to sew. I may have to

cook, I might mop the floor. But you help me, ba - by.

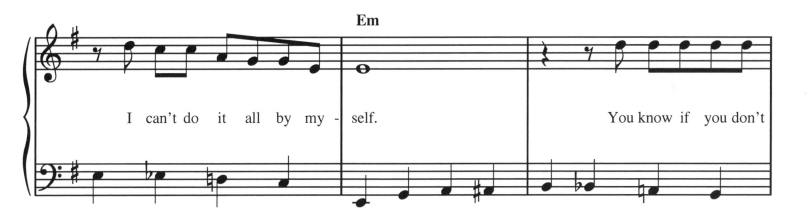

I can't do it all by my - self. You know if you don't

help me, dar - ling, _ I'll find my - self some-bod - y else.

When I walk, _____ you walk with me. And when I

Am

talk, you talk to me. _____ Oh, babe,

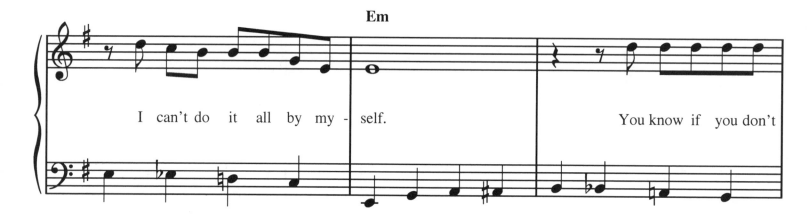

Em

I can't do it all by my - self. You know if you don't

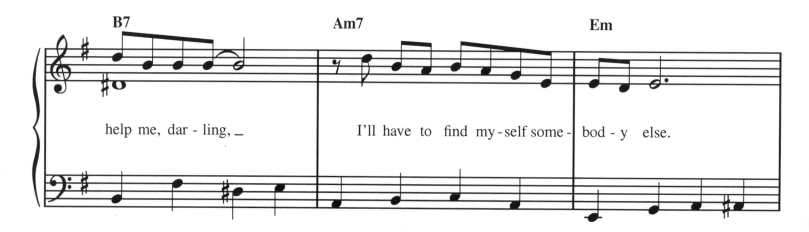

B7 Am7 Em

help me, dar - ling, _ I'll have to find my - self some - bod - y else.

I'M A MAN

By ELLAS McDANIEL

Man. The line I shoot

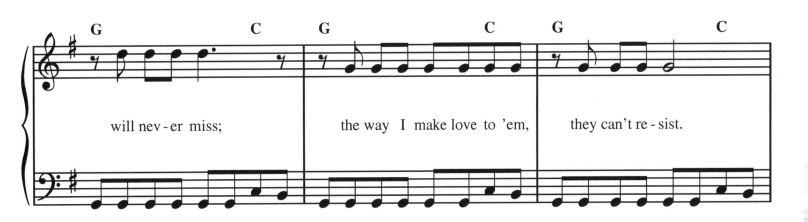

will nev - er miss; the way I make love to 'em, they can't re - sist.

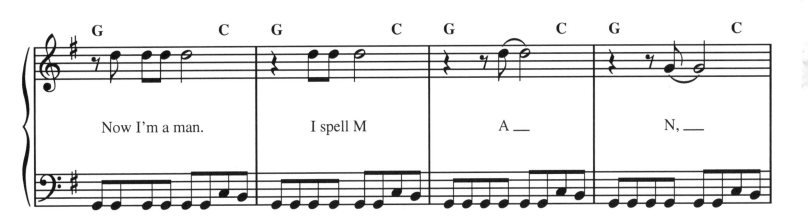

Now I'm a man. I spell M A — N, —

Man.

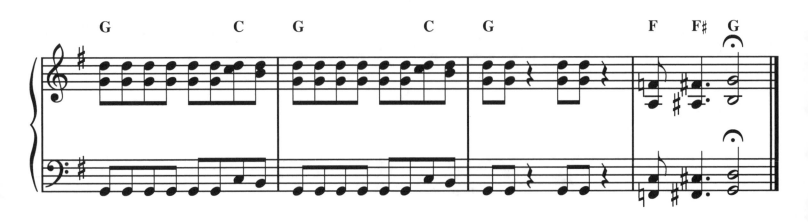

IN THE EVENING
(When The Sun Goes Down)

Words and Music by
LEROY CARR

62

IT'S A LOW DOWN DIRTY SHAME

Words and Music by
OLLIE SHEPARD

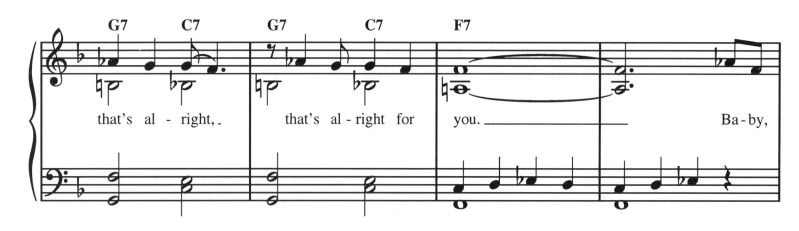

that's al - right,_ that's al - right for you._____ Ba - by,

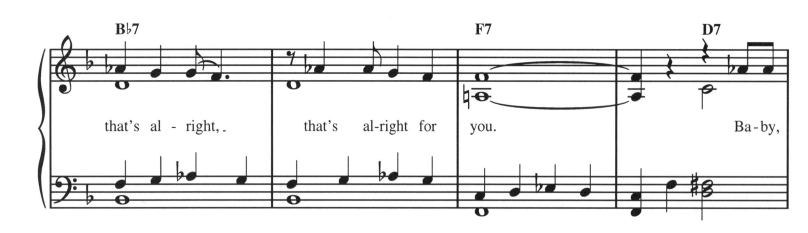

that's al - right,_ that's al-right for you._____ Ba - by,

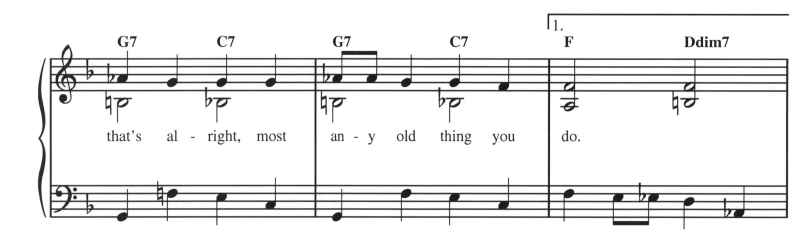

that's al - right, most an - y old thing you do.

It's a do.

MAD ABOUT HIM, SAD WITHOUT HIM, HOW CAN I BE GLAD WITHOUT HIM BLUES

Words and Music by LARRY MARKES
and DICK CHARLES

MCA music publishing

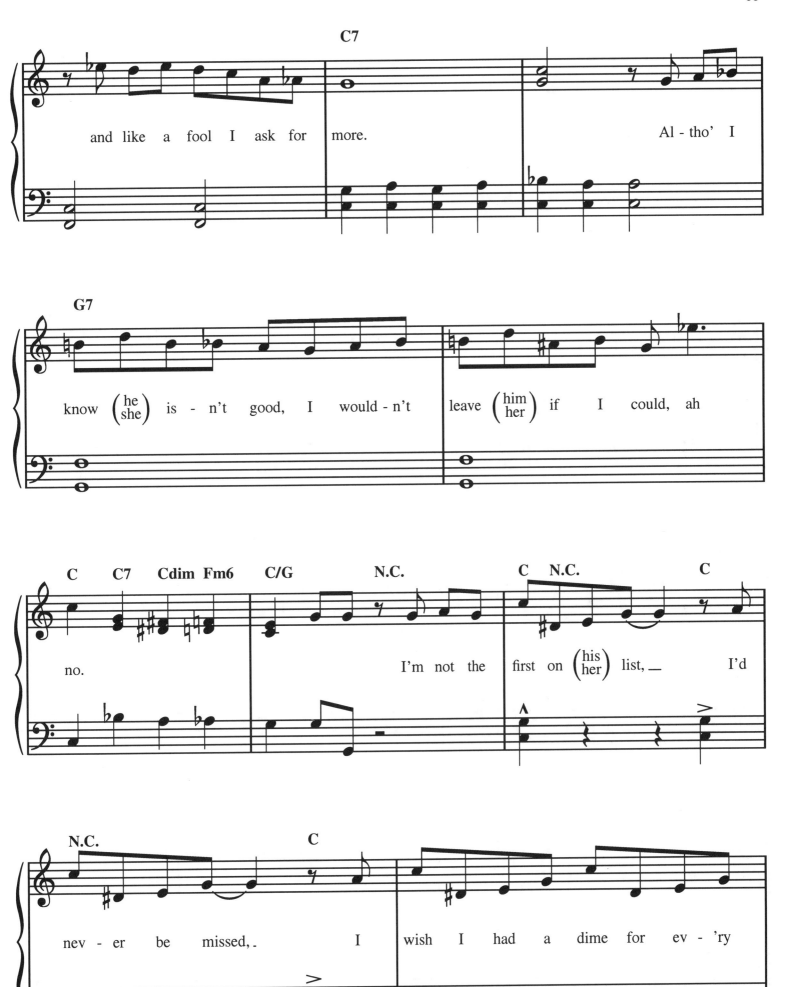

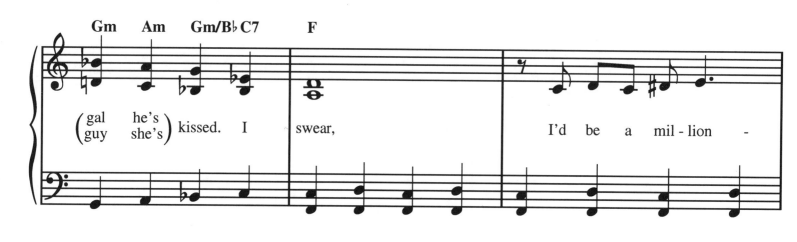

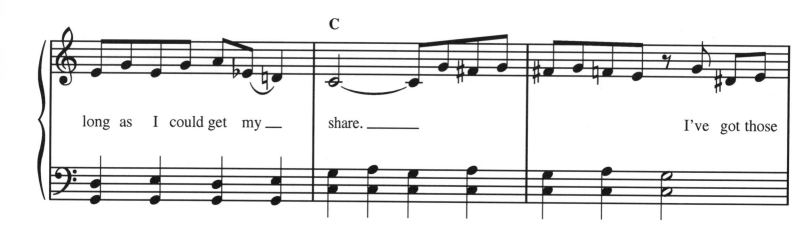

MEAN OLD WORLD

By WALTER JACOBS

74

MULE KICKING IN MY STALL

Words and Music by
McKinley MORGANFIELD

MEMPHIS BLUES

Words and Music by
W.C. HANDY

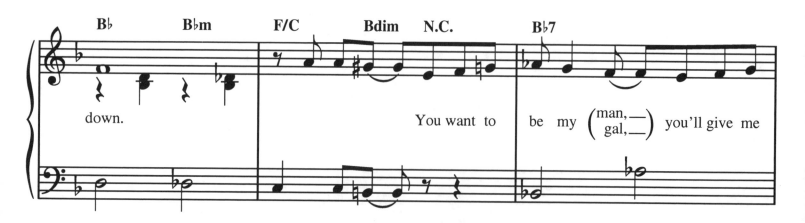

for - ty dol - lars down. If you don't

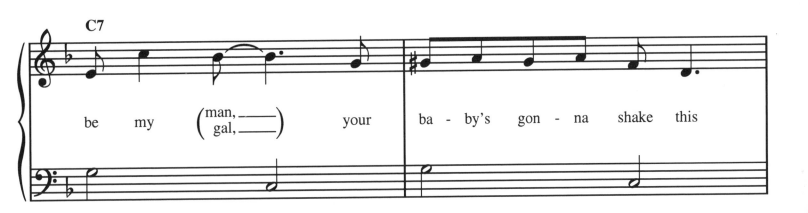

be my (man, gal,) your ba - by's gon - na shake this

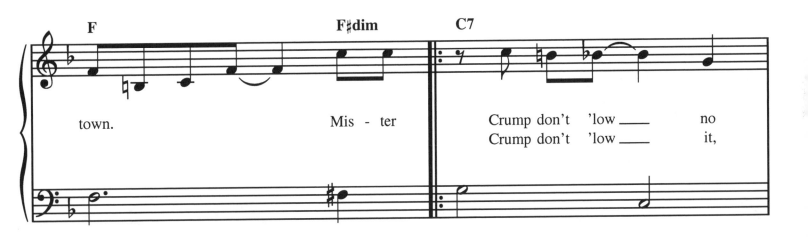

town. Mis - ter
Crump don't 'low ___ no
Crump don't 'low ___ it,

eas - y rid - ers here.
ain't goin' have _ it here.

Crump don't 'low ____ no
Crump don't 'low ____ it,

eas - y rid - ers
ain't goin' have ____ it

here.
here.

We don't care ___ what Mis - ter
Crump don't 'low, ___
we gon - na bar'l - house

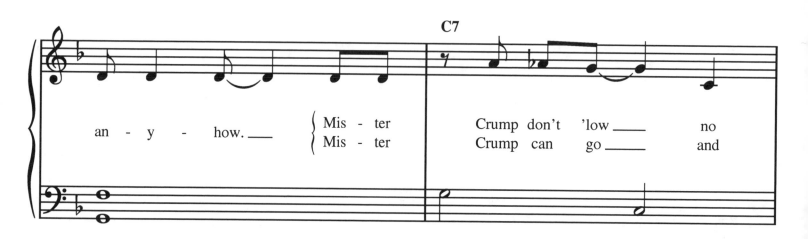

an - y - how. ___
Mis - ter
Mis - ter

Crump don't 'low ____ no
Crump can go ____ and

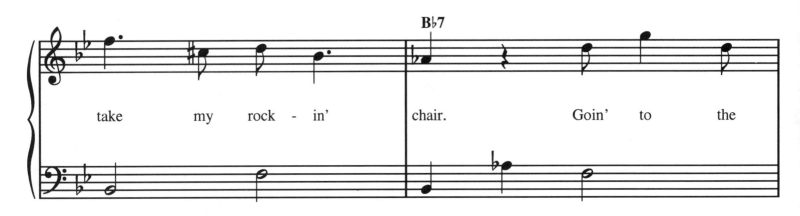

take my rock - in' chair. Goin' to the

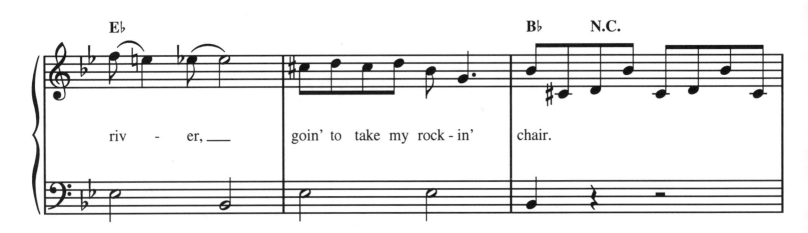

riv - er, ___ goin' to take my rock - in' chair.

Blues over - take me, goin' to rock a - way from

here. Oh, the Mis - sis - sip - pi Riv - er,

83

Mis - sis - sip - pi Riv - er so ____ deep an' wide, I said the

Mis - sis - sip - pi Riv - er's so ____ deep an' wide.

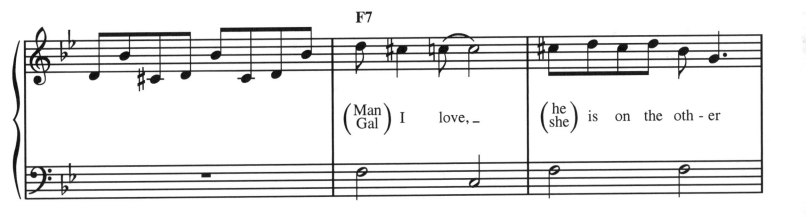

$\binom{\text{Man}}{\text{Gal}}$ I love, __ $\binom{\text{he}}{\text{she}}$ is on the oth - er

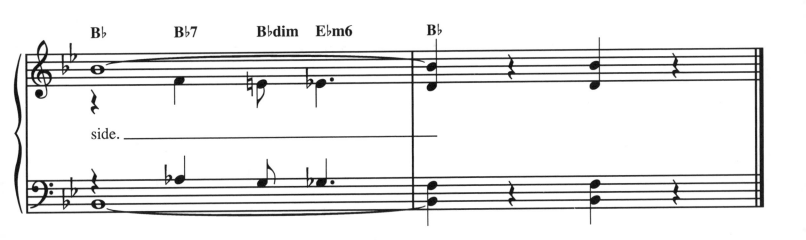

side. ____

MILK COW BLUES

Words and Music by
KOKOMO ARNOLD

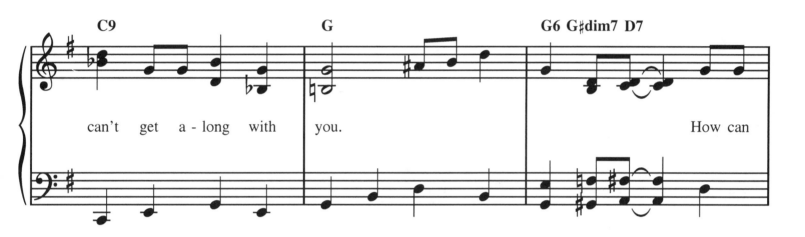

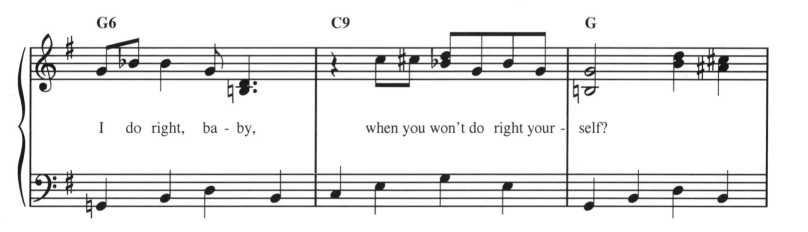

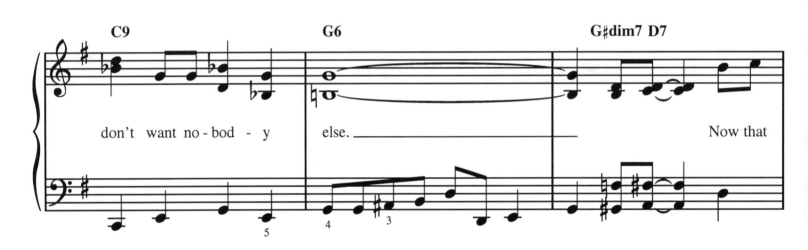

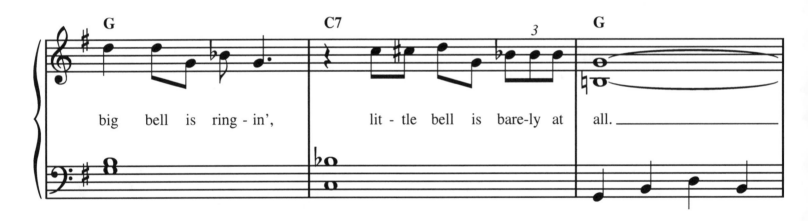

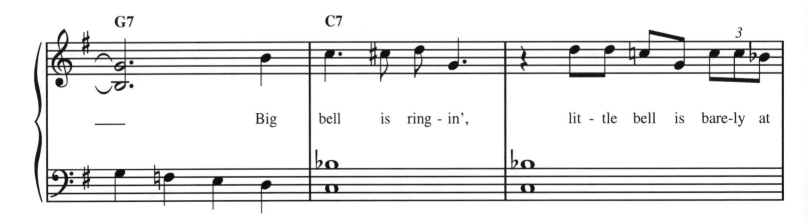

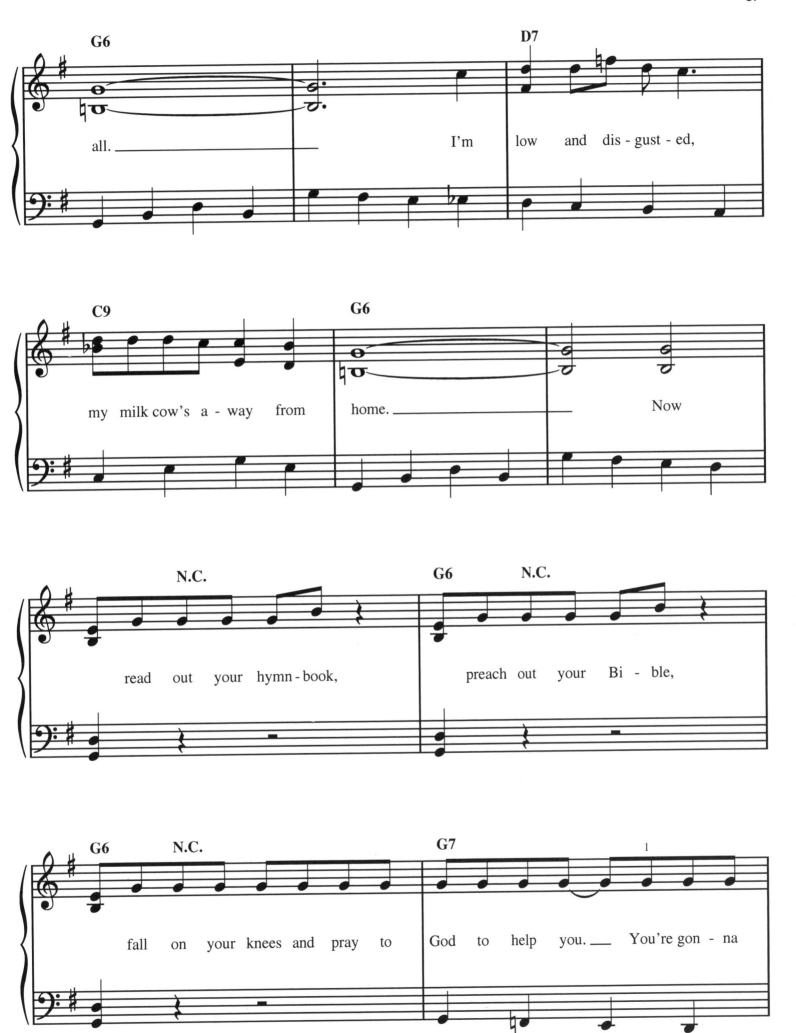

Additional Verses

2. My blues fell this mornin' and my love came falling down,
   My blues fell this mornin' and my love came falling down,
   I may be a low-down dog, mama, but please don't dog me around.

3. It takes a rockin' chair to rock, a rubber ball to roll,
   Takes a long, tall, sweet gal to satisfy my soul,
   Lord, I don't feel welcome, no place I go,
   'Cause the woman I love done throwed me from her door.

MY BABY LEFT ME

Words and Music by
ARTHUR CRUDUP

Additional Lyrics

3. Baby, one of these mornings, Lord, it won't be long.
   You'll look for me and, baby, and Daddy, he'll be gone.
   You know you left me, you know you left me.
   My baby even left me, never said goodbye.

4. Now, I stand at my window, wring my hands and moan.
   All I know is that the one I love is gone.
   My baby left me, you know she left me.
   My baby left me, never said a word.

PINETOP'S BLUES

Words and Music by
PINETOP SMITH

ST. LOUIS BLUES

Words and Music by
W.C. HANDY

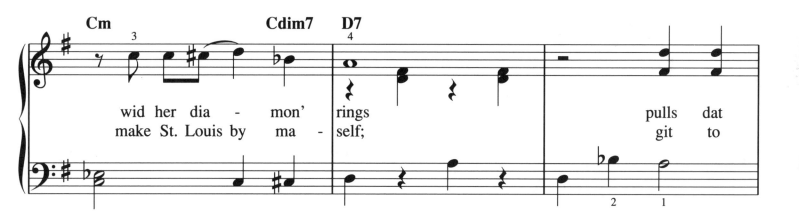

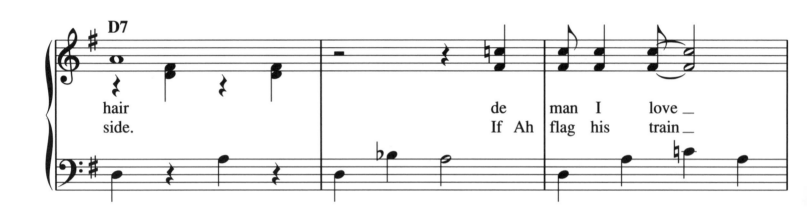

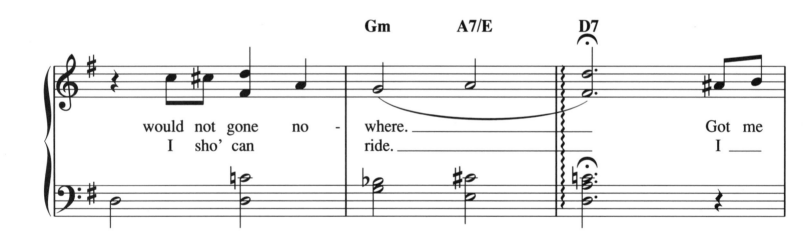

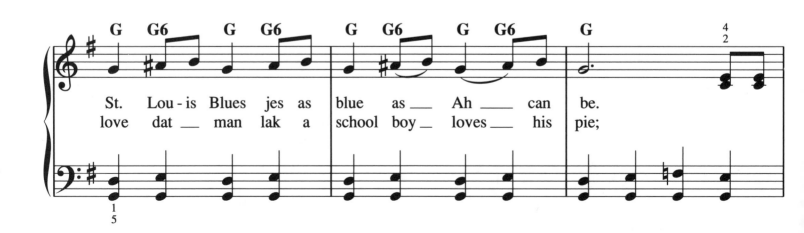

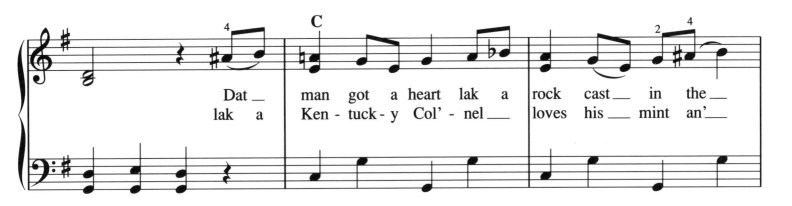

ROCK ME BABY

Words and Music by JOE JOSEA
and B.B. KING

Rock me, ba - by, rock me all ___ night long. ___
Rock me, ba - by, like you roll ___ a wa - gon wheel. _
Rock me, ba - by, hon - ey rock _ me slow. ___

SAINT JAMES INFIRMARY

Words and Music by
JOE PRIMROSE

sweet, so — cool — so fair. Went Blues.

Additional lyrics

2. Went up to see the doctor.
   "She's very low," he said.
   Went back to see my baby;
   Great God! She was lyin' there dead.

3. I went down to old Joe's bar-room
   On the corner by the square.
   They were servin' the drinks as usual,
   And the usual crowd was there.

4. On my left stood Joe McKennedy,
   His eyes blood-shot red.
   He turned to the crowd around him,
   These are the words he said:

5. Let her go, God bless her,
   Wherever she may be.
   She may search this wide world over,
   She'll never find a man like me.

6. Oh, when I die please bury me
   In my high-top Stetson hat.
   Put a gold piece on my watch chain
   So they'll know I died standin' pat.

7. Get six gamblers to carry my coffin,
   Six chorus girls to sing my song.
   Put a jazz band on my tail-gate
   To raise hell as we go along.

8. Now that's the end of my story;
   Let's have another round of booze.
   And if anyone should ask you, just tell them
   I've got the St. James Infirmary Blues.

SMOKESTACK LIGHTNING

By CHESTER BURNETT

hoo, _____ boo - hoo. _____

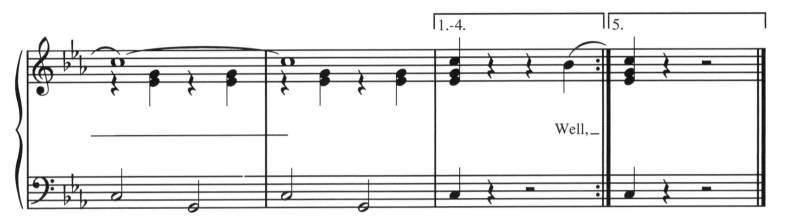

Well,_

Additional Lyrics

3. Well, tell me, baby,
Where did you stay last night?
Well, don't you hear me crying?
Boo-hoo, boo-hoo, boo-hoo.

4. Well, stop your train,
Let us go for a ride.
Well, don't you hear me crying?
Boo-hoo, boo-hoo, boo-hoo.

5. Well, fare thee well,
Never see you no more.
Well, don't you hear me crying?
Boo-hoo, boo-hoo, boo-hoo.

SUGAR BLUES

Words by LUCY FLETCHER
Music by CLARENCE WILLIAMS

MCA music publishing

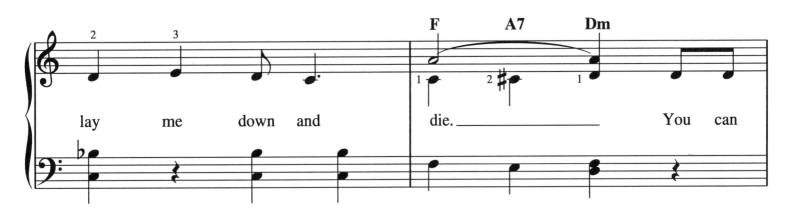

TAIN'T NOBODY'S BIZ-NESS
IF I DO

Words and Music by PORTER GRAINGER
and EVERETT ROBBINS

MCA music publishing

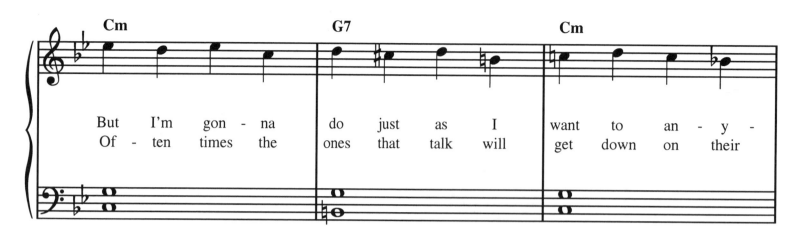

But I'm gon - na / do just as I / want to an - y -
Of - ten times the / ones that talk will / get down on their

way, / and don't care / if they all de -
knees / and beg you / par - don for their

spise / me. / If I should
squawk - in'. / If I dis -

take a no - tion / to jump in / to _____ the o - cean
like my lov - er / and leave him / for _____ an - oth - er,

biz - ness   if ____ I ____   do. ____

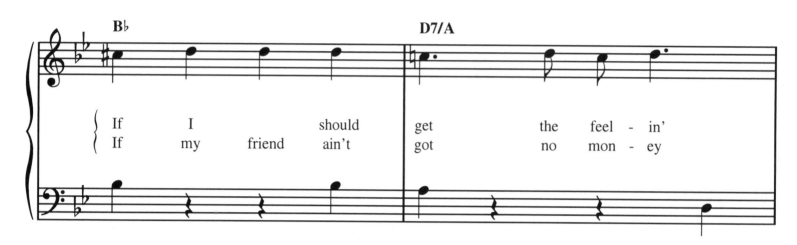

If   I   should   get   the   feel - in'
If   my   friend   ain't   got   no   mon - ey

to   dance   up -   on ____   the   ceil - in'
and   I   say,   "Take   all   mine,   hon - ey,"

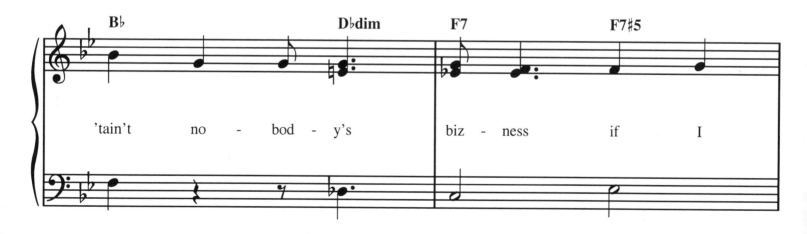

'tain't   no - bod - y's   biz - ness   if   I

TOBACCO ROAD

Words and Music by
JOHN D. LOUDERMILK

in the mid - dle of To - bac - co Road. _____ Wo wo
bring it back _ to To - bac - co Road. _____ Wo wo

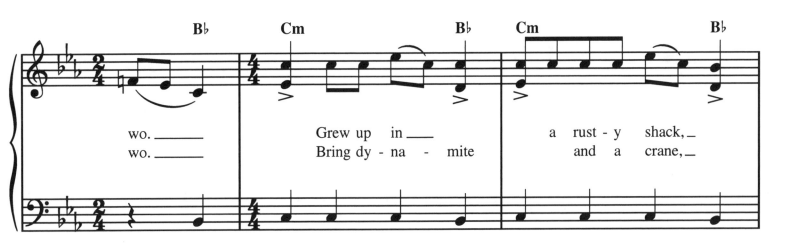

wo. _____ Grew up in _____ a rust - y shack, _
wo. _____ Bring dy - na - mite and a crane, _

all I had was hang-in' on my back. On - ly you _ know
blow it up start all o - ver a - gain. Build a town, _ be

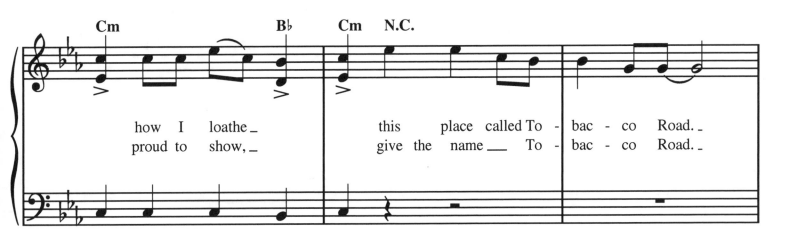

how I loathe _ this place called To - bac - co Road. _
proud to show, _ give the name _ To - bac - co Road. _

but I love you | Tobacco 'cos you're home.

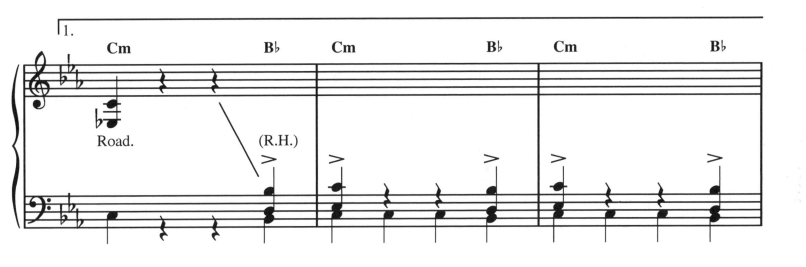

Road. (R.H.)

Repeat and Fade

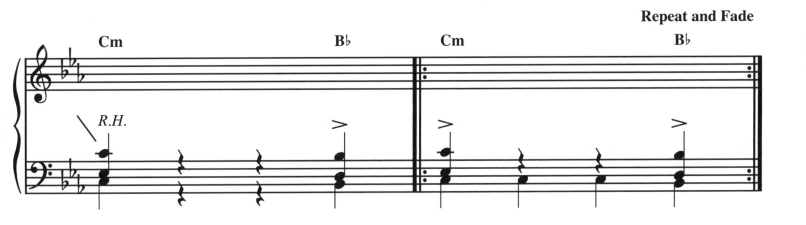

R.H.

THE THRILL IS GONE

Words and Music by ROY HAWKINS
and RICK DARNELL

WHY I SING THE BLUES

Words and Music by
B.B. KING

MCA music publishing

122

been a-round a long time, I real-ly have paid my dues. _____

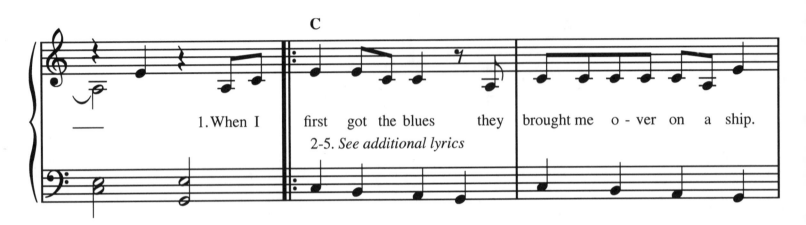

_____ 1. When I first got the blues they brought me o-ver on a ship.
2-5. *See additional lyrics*

Men were stand-ing o-ver me and a lot more with the whip. And ev'-ry - bod-y wan-na know

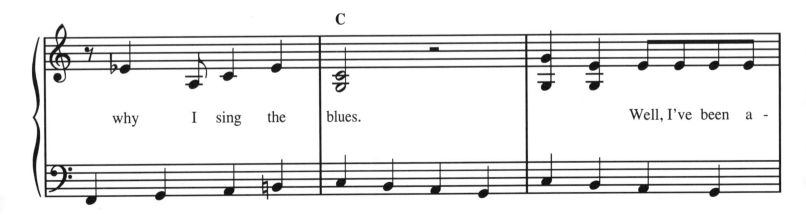

why I sing the blues. Well, I've been a-

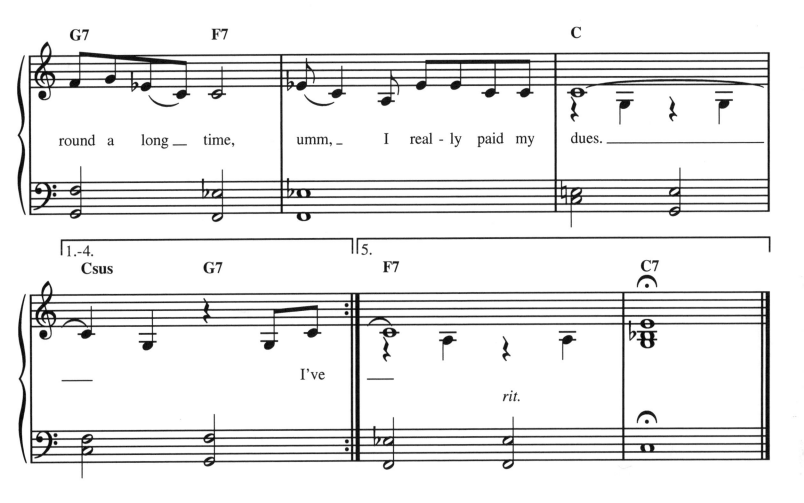

Additional Lyrics

2. I've laid in the ghetto flats, cold and numb.
   I heard the rats tell the bedbugs to give the roaches some,
   and ev'rybody wanna know why I sing the blues.
   Well I've been around a long time, Umm, I really paid my dues.

3. I stood in line down in the county hall.
   I heard a man say we are going to build some new apartments for y'all.
   (And) ev'rybody wanna know why I sing the blues.
   Well, I've been around a long time, Umm, I really paid my dues.

4. My kid's gonna grow up, gonna grow to be a fool,
   'Cause they ain't got no more room, no more for him in school.
   And everybody wants to know why I sing the blues.
   I say, I've been around a long time, yes, I've really paid my dues.

5. Yea, you know the company told me, yes, you're born to lose.
   Everybody around feel it, seems like everybody's got the blues.
   But I had them a long time, I really, really paid my dues.
   You know I ain't ashamed of it, people, I just love to sing the blues.

WEST END BLUES

Words and Music by JOE OLIVER
and CLARENCE WILLIAMS

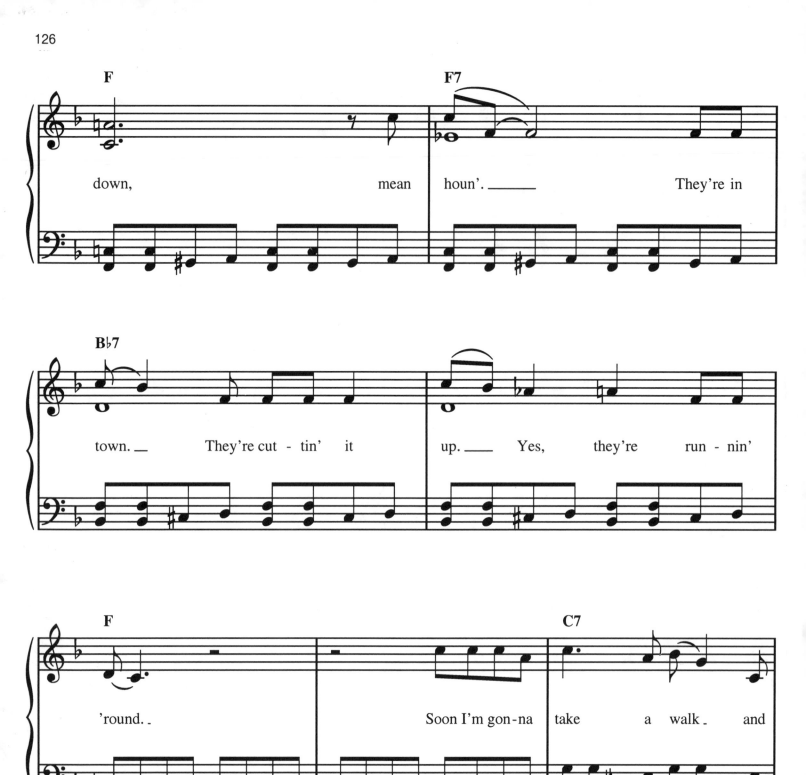

down,   mean   houn'. _____   They're in

town. __   They're cut - tin' it   up. ____ Yes, they're   run - nin'

'round. .   Soon I'm gon-na   take   a   walk _ and

knock   up - on ____   her   door. _____

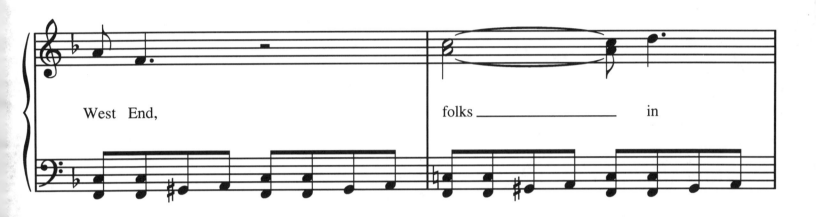